FAST FORWARD

Shipwreck

illustrated by

Peter Dennis

BARRON'S

Contents

Introduction

Imagine you are on board a Spanish galleon, hundreds of years ago. There is noise and confusion as the crew hurry to load her up with silver and gold from the Americas. Tomorrow she sets sail for Spain! The sailors make sure they have enough supplies of food and drink. The captain welcomes a nobleman and his wife aboard. And the guards prepare to defend the ship and its precious cargo from the dangers that may lie ahead ...

The story told in this book is like a journey. It is not a journey from one place to another (for the ship's great voyage, as we shall see, is cut unexpectedly short), but one in which you travel through time. With each turn of the page, the date moves forward a few hours, years or even centuries. Each time—every stop on your journey—is like a new chapter in the life of the ship. The early days in the shipyard when it is built, its short, glorious life on the Spanish Main, its capture at the hands of the pirates, and its long years as a wreck at the bottom of the sea—all tell the story of the galleon.

Look out for the ship's carpenter, an important member of the crew. Wearing his distinctive green cap, he appears in many of the illustrations.

Use this thumb index to travel though time! Just find the page you want to see and flip it open. This way you can make a quick comparison between one scene and another, even though some show events that took place some years apart. A little black arrow on the page points to the time of the scene illustrated on that page.

The masts, sails and rigging (ropes and pulleys attached to the masts and sails) of a galleon were not added until the ship was ready to launch. The masts fitted into holes in the deck, and were secured with ropes running down the ship's sides.

Treenail mooter

Caulker

Mold-loft

Consulting plans

Curved timbers

Carpenter carves figurehead

Tar boilers

The 1630s

In a shipyard in Spain, workmen are busy building a galleon, a large ocean-going sailing ship. In the mold-loft, carpenters use patterns from the floor to mark out shapes on pieces of timber. These pieces are then cut to size in the sawpits. Curved timbers are joined together to make the frames or "ribs" of the ship. After that, the treenail mooters fix planks of wood to the frames with wooden pins (treenails), to form the outside shell of the ship.

Caulkers fill and waterproof the gaps between the planks by hammering in rope fibers and coating them with hot tar, or pitch. Rope-makers twist thin strands of rope together to fashion thick, strong ropes, while in the forge blacksmiths cast iron bolts and nails.

Timber

Sawpit

Rope-making

Frames

Forge

Sails

Mast

Captain's
quarters

Pulley

Food
stores

TREASURES OF THE SPANISH MAIN

After Christopher Columbus, in the service of Spain, landed in the Americas in 1492, Spain claimed much of Central and South America as its own. This area, and eventually the whole of the Caribbean Sea and its islands, became known as the Spanish Main. The existing Native American civilizations were wiped out and their vast stocks of gold and silver were shipped back to Spain. But the sea journey was threatened by pirates and privateers, who sought to steal Spain's treasure.

Guards

A year later ...

The galleon is in a port on the Spanish Main. The crew is loading it with treasure to take back to Spain. They use winches or pulley systems attached to the masts to haul up the heaviest chests. Guards keep watch on the treasure while it is on the quayside.

Stores of food, fresh water, beer and wine are also loaded, tightly sealed in wooden barrels. These will be the only source of food and drink for the sailors until they arrive back in Spain.

The 1630s

A year later

Crow's nest

Cannon

Sails

Stores

A day later ...

The galleon has left port, and is in full sail on its way back to Spain. Some of the crew rest in their bunks while others are hard at work cleaning out the cannons and adjusting the sails. Below deck, the helmsman steers the ship using a whipstaff, a long lever that moves the rudder at the back of the ship.

Sails

Climbing the rigging

Pirate boat

Crew in bunks

Cleaning cannons

In the galley, the cook and his assistant prepare a meal for the captain. A guard stands at the door to the treasure store. On deck, off-duty Spanish soldiers enjoy some music, while the ship's carpenter repairs a flight of steps. A noble passenger and his wife admire the view.

Only a few of the crew notice the approaching fleet of small pirate boats, but it is too late to sound the alarm.

The 1630s

A year later

A day later

Nobleman and his wife

Captain's quarters

Lady's maid

Helmsman

Whipstaff

Guard

Treasure

Galley

Some pirates used small boats known as *piraguas* to raid ships in coastal waters.

Pirate boats

11

A few minutes later ...

The pirates swarm onto the ship, brandishing their weapons—pistols, muskets, cutlasses and daggers. The soldiers rush to grab their own weapons while the crew fight back with whatever comes to hand. Within moments, there is complete chaos on board ship. The nobleman, his wife and her maid look on with terror.

The pirates charge below decks in search of treasure and supplies, including weapons, food and drink. They attack the crew and guards before they have time to arm themselves.

Cutlass

Musket

ON BECOMING A PIRATE

While privateers were employed by foreign governments to attack treasure ships, most "true" pirates were out to take everything they captured. Many pirates had once been ordinary sailors who found that they could make much more money as pirates. Others were runaway slaves, adventurers and outlaws. Some, known as buccaneers, had been wild pig and cattle hunters on Hispaniola, a Caribbean island. They turned to piracy after being forced off the island by the Spanish. A few pirates were women, who fought just as eagerly as the men.

Some pirates patroled coastal waters, using small Caribbean islands from which to launch their small, swift boats upon unsuspecting Spanish galleons. Others bought or stole larger ships, which could make longer journeys out to sea. When Spanish treasure ships began to sail in groups for protection, the pirates were forced to attack ships in port. Some could still use speed and cunning to capture a galleon.

The 1630s

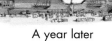

A year later

A day later

A few minutes later

Two hours later ...

The fighting is over, and the pirates are victorious. Many Spanish guards have been killed. The pirates tie up the crew, or hold them under armed guard while they empty the galleon of as much treasure as they can find. The captain and his officers are thrown overboard to the sharks. One pirate boat takes away the wealthy passengers to be held for ransom, as well as some of the crew who will be sold as slaves.

Loading up supplies

14

The pirates take treasure such as gold and silver from the galleon. They also load up their boats with food, drink, weapons and ammunition, medicines, sailcloth, ropes and even items of furniture. They sometimes take the ship itself, but this large, heavy galleon is of no use to them, so they decide to sink it.

The pirates attach barrels of gunpowder to the side of the ship. When their companions are well clear of the galleon, the last few pirates will light the fuse and row away as fast as they can before the barrels blow up.

Crew taken prisoner

Attaching barrels of gunpowder to the ship

Lowering treasure into a boat

Pirate boat takes away prisoners

Crew allowed to escape by boat

The 1630s

A year later

A day later

A few minutes later

Two hours later

Spanish money, minted on the Spanish Main and then shipped to Spain, was of particular interest to the pirates. Gold doubloons were highly prized, but silver coins known as "pieces of eight" were also very valuable. Some lucky pirates became rich beyond their wildest dreams.

A little while later ...

The pirates have brought their haul of treasure, weapons and supplies to the shore, where they divide them up.

Galleon

Pirate boats

Pirate captain

Signing ransom

They celebrate their victory with a barbecue of wild pig meat, a skill they have learned from local Indian tribes. The pirate captain forces the nobleman and his wife to sign a ransom note for their safe release. As the last pirate boats reach the island, the galleon explodes.

THE PIRATE CODE

Before they could join a pirate band, new recruits had to promise to follow a strict code of conduct. This included fighting with enthusiasm in battle and keeping their weapons in good working order. There were penalties for disobeying these rules. Stealing from shipmates and deserting the ship were the most serious crimes. Disgraced pirates could be abandoned on a desert island, or even put to death.

Before a battle, the whole crew discussed its plan of attack, with any disagreements settled by a vote. The ship's captain could be overthrown by a show of hands questioning his leadership. The pirates even received money if they suffered any injuries while they were fighting for the band.

Treasure was divided up according to an agreed system. The captain and his officers received slightly larger shares than the rest of the crew. Some pirates became rich and retired to a life of luxury, but many spent any money they earned on drink and gambling within days of arriving in port.

The 1630s

A year later

A day later

A few minutes later

Two hours later

A little while later

Drunken pirate

Barbecue

17

Some hours later ...

The wrecked galleon rests on the sea bed. A gaping hole has been blasted in its side by the force of the exploding gunpowder. Water now fills the ship, causing light objects to float out of the hole. In one small storeroom lies a treasure chest that has been overlooked by the pirates. Some heavy items, such as cannons and barrels of food, fell out of the ship as it sank, and now rest on the sandy sea bed.

Most of the crew of the galleon are either dead or held captive by the pirates. But a few survivors have managed to clamber up into the crow's nest. As they sit and hope that a passing ship will come to their rescue, hungry sharks circle in the water below ...

Fallen mast

A DANGEROUS LIFE

There were many ways in which a 17th-century ship could be wrecked. Apart from being sunk in battle, ships could be overbalanced by a badly-loaded cargo or heavy winds. Some were poorly designed: their own tall, top-heavy shape made them overturn in the wind. Out at sea, storms could whip up huge waves that would swamp a ship. Closer to shore, sharp coral reefs or rocks might lie just below the water's surface.

Sometimes shipwrecked sailors were able to escape in rowing boats or on makeshift rafts. But many drowned for one simple reason: very few sailors could actually swim.

Crow's nest

Treasure chest

The 1630s

A year later

A day later

A few minutes later

Two hours later

A little while later

Some hours later

19

A year later...

The few survivors of the shipwreck have returned to Spain with reports on the whereabouts of the sunken ship. In the hope of finding what treasure and weapons remain, the government has sent a salvage ship to the site. The ship is run and crewed by Spaniards, but the divers are African and Indian slaves.

The slaves dive into the water with bags to carry small items. They use ropes and grappling irons for larger treasures. Although some parts of the wreck are beginning to rot away, the divers are able to swim inside. One has found a cannon. He ties it to a rope, which is then winched up to the salvage ship by slaves walking inside a treadwheel.

The divers cannot work underwater for long, as they have to come to the surface to breathe. A treadwheel lowers one slave in a diving bell full of air. This allows him to stay underwater for as long as the air lasts.

People can only hold their breath underwater for a minute or so. An invention called a diving bell allowed early divers to work underwater for longer periods. In some designs, such as John Lethbridge's diving barrel *(above)*, the diver relied on the supply of air inside the bell, which could last up to half an hour. Other diving bells contained an air pipe to pump fresh air down from the surface.

Slave with grappling iron

Treadwheels

Salvage ship

Winching up cannon

Diving bell

Treasure chest

The 1630s

A year later

A day later

A few minutes later

Two hours later

A little while later

Some hours later

A year later

21

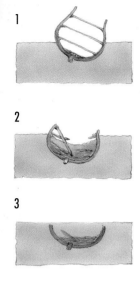

200 years later ...

The site of the shipwreck has become part of a coral reef, teeming with life. Ocean currents have covered much of the ship in a layer of sand and mud. Beneath this layer there is no oxygen, so materials such as cloth, wood or leather, which would otherwise rot away or be eaten by marine worms, are preserved.

Only a few pottery jars and metal objects such as a cannon, a treasure chest and the ship's anchor remain above the sea bed. They gradually become

When a wooden ship sinks (1), water currents gradually wash sediment (silt, sand and mud) from the sea bed into the ship's hull (2). Any timbers left uncovered are gradually eaten away by marine organisms such as shipworms, which are found in most ocean waters. The weakened timbers collapse, and eventually the entire shipwreck is covered in layers of sediment (3).

Coral

Cannon

encrusted with coral and the shells of tiny sea creatures. Rust, formed by sea water reacting with objects made of iron, has built up on the anchor and on the treasure chest. Concretions, lumps of rust that grow bigger and bigger, have started to form.

Colorful coral reef fish swim over the buried ship, hunting for tiny creatures among the coral. They are ready to hide if a cruising moray eel, shark or ray gets too close. Meanwhile, the wreck of the galleon sleeps on, lost and forgotten beneath the sea bed ...

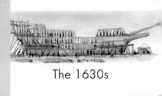

The 1630s

A year later

A day later

A few minutes later

Two hours later

A little while later

Some hours later

A year later

200 years later

Ray

Moray eel

Shark

Treasure chest

Pottery jars

A few years ago ...

Even with modern-day diving equipment, divers are not able to swim down to very deep wrecks. They risk getting "the bends"—bubbles of nitrogen that form in the blood when deep-water divers rise to the surface. At great depths, their bodies could also be crushed by the pressure of the water. Instead, up to two divers can use a small under-water vehicle called a submersible. Submersibles have thick walls to withstand water pressure. They are equipped with lights, cameras and often a long arm, controlled by the crew, which can pick up objects from a wreck. Propellers help to move the submersible in all directions.

After studying historical records and scanning the sea bed with detection equipment, a team of divers has finally discovered the shipwreck. There is little to be seen above the sea bed, but metal detectors tell them that there is iron, bronze, or even silver or gold below the coral and sand. The divers are careful not to disturb the site until they can set up a proper archaeological survey to record where they find objects.

Research vessel

Dolphin

Cutlass

Metal detector

Anchor

Turtles

Cannon

FINDING A WRECK

While some shipwreck hunters hope to find long-lost treasure, archaeologists are more interested in what shipwrecks can tell them about life in the past. Clothing and equipment can give a valuable "snapshot" of life at the time the ship went down. Unfortunately, some shipwrecks, especially those that went down in shallow waters, have already been plundered by treasure hunters over the centuries.

Finding a shipwreck can be a long and difficult task. Historical documents and charts are often the only source of information about the location of a sunken ship, and they are often inaccurate and vague. But once in the right area, research vessels can pinpoint the shipwreck exactly using detection equipment such as sonar—which locates objects using sound waves—and magnetometers, which can detect metal objects below several layers of sediment.

The 1630s

A year later

A day later

A few minutes later

Two hours later

A little while later

Some hours later

A year later

200 years later

A few years ago

A year later ...

Divers are carrying out a full-scale archaeological investigation on the shipwreck site. They set up a grid of poles that divide the site into squares, to record where items are found. The poles also help them to avoid standing on the wreck. The divers clear away the thick sediment covering the wreck using suction pipes called air lifts. Old timbers, preserved for centuries below the mud, are revealed, along with pottery, cannons and even a mysterious chest.

The native peoples of Central and South America were superb craftsmen. They held treasure troves of beautifully-made ornaments, statues and jewelry made of gold. When the Spanish settlers arrived, they melted down many of these riches into coins or bars, and their historical value was lost forever.

A signal given by a metal detector can be the only clue to a precious item hidden beneath the sea bed. The sediment can then be brushed away to reveal an exciting find.

Research vessel

Lifting bags

Diver taking photograph

Remains of ship's timbers

Grid of poles

Treasure chest

Before moving any find, divers record its position using tape measures, label it and make sketches. They video the site, as well as taking photographs that can be put together by computers to create a map of the whole site.

Finally, the finds can be taken to the surface. Small items are placed into baskets and lifted by air-filled balloons (lifting bags), but heavy metal objects such as cannons have to be winched up from the research vessel above.

Raising a cannon

Recording

Air lift

Sketching the site

Video camera

The 1630s

A year later

A day later

A few minutes later

Two hours later

A little while later

Some hours later

A year later

200 years later

A few years ago

A year later

27

Today

The *Vasa* was a Swedish warship that sank on its maiden (first) voyage in 1628, even before it had left the harbor. The cold Baltic Sea preserved the ship so well that it could be raised and restored almost completely.

The *Mary Rose*, a large English warship, sank off the coast of Britain in 1545 and lay almost forgotten until it was rediscovered in 1967. Thousands of items were found on board, from clothing and cooking equipment to longbows and musical instruments. The hull itself was raised in 1982, and after years of spraying with water and preserving chemicals, is now on display in a museum.

Actor

Captain's quarters

Helmsman

Cook

Gunners

Ticket office

A replica of the galleon is on display at a holiday resort in Spain. Visitors crowd the ship, imagining what it must have been like to be a sailor or a pirate. Actors in costume describe life on board ship, while waxwork models of the crew portray them carrying out their daily tasks. One of them seems very familiar ...

BRINGING A WRECK TO LIFE

Once items from a shipwreck are brought to the surface, conserving work begins. Stone or glass may just need to be cleaned, but materials such as cloth, leather and wood are treated with chemicals to prevent them from breaking apart as they dry out.

Sometimes the timbers of the ship itself are raised. Special lifting equipment must be used to support every part of the ship. Once out of the water, the ship must be continually sprayed with water and a waxy chemical called PEG, a process that can take years.

The structure of the ship and the items discovered are studied by historical experts, who are able to build up a picture of life on board hundreds of years ago. Many items are copied to be displayed in museums, so that the fragile originals can be kept in a stable environment.

Guards

Crew's quarters

Sailmaker

Barrel-maker

29 ▶

The 1630s

A year later

A day later

A few minutes later

Two hours later

A little while later

Some hours later

A year later

200 years later

A few years ago

A year later

Today

Glossary

Archaeologist Someone who studies human life from the past, using the evidence from finds buried in the ground or at sea.

Buccaneers Former hunters who turned to piracy after being driven from the Caribbean island of Hispaniola by the Spanish.

Cargo The goods carried on board a ship.

Caulkers Workmen who sealed the joints between planks on a ship by hammering greased rope fibers into the joints, and then covering them with hot tar.

Crow's nest A lookout platform around a ship's mast.

Deserting Leaving a ship permanently, without permission.

Diving bell A device that allows divers to breathe air while underwater.

Helmsman The sailor who steers the ship.

Galleon A type of large sailing ship used for warfare and trading between the 15th and 18th centuries.

Galley The kitchen of a ship.

Grappling iron A hook with several prongs, attached to a rope and used for holding onto or lifting objects.

Hull The main outer body of a ship.

Jolly Roger The flag flown by a pirate ship.

Magnetometer A device that uses magnetic forces to find and map metal objects, even under the sea bed.

Musket A gun with a long barrel, similar to a rifle, used between the 16th and 18th centuries.

Pieces of eight The pirate name for Spanish silver coins, worth eight reals each (real means "royal").

Pirate Someone who attacks ships and steals their contents. There are still pirates around today.

Privateer Someone employed by the government of one country to attack ships belonging to another.

Ransom A sum of money paid to a kidnapper for the release of the victim.

Rudder A flat board at the back of a ship that is moved from side to side to change the ship's direction.

Salvage Retrieving the contents of a shipwreck.

Slaves People whose freedom has been taken away. They have to work for the people who "own" them.

Sonar A method of navigation and detection under water. Sound waves are sent out, and the echoes that bounce back are used to locate objects.

Spanish Main The parts of Central and South America and the Caribbean islands that were claimed by Spain after Christopher Columbus discovered America in 1492.

Submersible A small submarine.

Whipstaff The long lever used to steer a ship.